COURAGEO

INSPIRING BOOKS FOR KIDS 8–12 SHAPING BOYS INTO LEADERS

Riley Stone

First Edition

ISBN: 9798872759911

CONTENTS

INTRODUCTION

Embark on an extraordinary voyage! Picture the greatest explorers, venturing into the vastness of space or navigating the mysteries of ancient lands. Just like these adventurers, life's journey is packed with thrills and challenges. It's said that stars shine brightest in the darkest of nights, and similarly, our inner strength is forged in the moments we dare to step beyond comfort. Each boy's heart harbors a seed of potential, craving the nurturing rays of guidance and the waters of wisdom to sprout into a leader.

Join us as we follow a band of courageous boys on their quest. Through joy and adversity, triumphs and trials, they sculpt their paths. They'll encounter moments of elation, sparks of frustration, and crossroads cloaked in hesitation. Yet, with every step, they gather the essence of leadership: learning to harness the power of empathy, wield the sword of integrity, and wear the armor of perseverance.

Leadership, after all, isn't a gift bestowed to the few; it's a flame that can be kindled in the heart of every boy. True courage doesn't roar; it is the quiet voice at day's end whispering, "I will try again tomorrow." It's about standing tall in the face of adversity, embracing challenges as opportunities to rise, and illuminating the way for others.

So, let's turn the page and venture into a realm where bravery crafts legends, and every tale inspires a future leader. Are you ready to guide these boys on their path to becoming the heroes of their own stories?

In the heart of the vast, sparkling ocean, there was an island unlike any other. This was no ordinary island; it was a hidden paradise, bursting with colorful flowers, mysterious caves, and chirping tropical birds. In the center of this enchanting island stood a lively pirate village, and it was here that young pirate Henry called home.

Henry, with his trusty parrot Skippy perched on his shoulder, stood at the helm of his rugged pirate ship, gazing out at the endless sea. The sun danced on the waves, casting a golden glow on his face.

"Skippy," Henry said thoughtfully, his eyes scanning the horizon, "there's more to this world than just our island, you know. I can feel it."

Skippy, a bright green parrot with a mischievous twinkle in his eye, ruffled his feathers. "Squawk! More to see, more to find, Henry!" he squawked in agreement.

As the day turned to dusk, the duo returned to the island, their minds filled with dreams of adventure. That night, under a canopy of twinkling stars, the pirates gathered around a crackling fire, sharing tales of legendary treasures and uncharted waters.

In the midst of the laughter and storytelling, Henry's curiosity grew. He knew that there was a world of secrets just waiting to be discovered. And as fate would have it, his chance to uncover one was closer than he ever imagined.

The next morning, while cleaning the ship, Henry stumbled upon a hidden compartment he had never noticed before. Inside, covered in a fine layer of dust, was an old, worn-out map.

"Skippy, look at this!" Henry exclaimed, his eyes wide with excitement.

Skippy flew over, peering at the map with interest. "Squawk! A map! What does it show, Henry?"

"It looks like... it's a map to Pirate's Cove!" Henry gasped, his heart racing. Pirate's Cove was the stuff of legends, rumored to be the resting place of the greatest treasure ever known.

The duo examined the map closely, tracing the path marked out in faded ink. It wound through treacherous seas, past mysterious landmarks, leading to a spot marked with an 'X'.

"We have to find this treasure, Skippy," Henry declared, his voice filled with determination. "It could be the greatest adventure of our lives!"

Skippy flapped his wings excitedly. "Squawk! Adventure awaits, Henry! Adventure awaits!"

With the map as their guide, Henry and Skippy prepared to embark on a journey unlike any they had ever taken. Little did they know, their quest for the lost treasure of Pirate's Cove would be filled with challenges, surprises, and a rival pirate who would stop at nothing to claim the treasure for himself.
As the first light of dawn crept over the horizon, Henry and Skippy were already bustling around the ship, preparing for their grand adventure. The crew, a band of hearty pirates with a love for the sea, watched in awe as Henry explained the plan.

"We're off to find the lost treasure of Pirate's Cove!" Henry announced, his eyes sparkling with excitement. "This map will lead us there, but it won't be easy. We'll face challenges like we've never seen before!"

The crew erupted into cheers, ready for the adventure. They quickly set to work, hoisting sails and securing supplies, their spirits high.

As they sailed into the open sea, the clear skies and calm waters seemed like a good omen. Skippy perched on the crow's nest, keeping a sharp eye out.

"Squawk! Smooth sailing, Henry!" Skippy called down.

Henry smiled, feeling the cool sea breeze in his hair. "It's perfect, Skippy. But we must stay alert. Pirate's Cove is full of mysteries."

The adventure took a turn when dark clouds gathered on the horizon, and the calm sea began to churn. A storm was brewing, and it was coming fast.

"Hold tight!" Henry shouted over the roaring wind. The crew scrambled, securing ropes and battening down hatches as the ship plunged into the heart of the storm.

Lightning cracked across the sky, illuminating the fierce waves that threatened to swallow them whole. Henry stood steadfast at the helm, steering with all his might.

"We can do this!" he yelled, his voice barely audible over the storm's fury.

With determination and teamwork, they navigated through the tempest, emerging on the other side with their ship intact but their nerves shaken.

As they continued their journey, the challenges didn't end with the storm. One day, while passing through a narrow strait, a giant sea creature emerged from the depths, its eyes as big as saucers.

The crew panicked, but Henry remained calm. "Don't harm it! It's just curious!" he instructed.

Following Henry's lead, they navigated carefully around the creature, which, after a few tense moments, disappeared back into the deep.

The days turned into weeks, and their journey was filled with both wonders and dangers. They encountered islands with strange, singing birds and navigated through waters glowing with bioluminescent creatures.

But their greatest challenge came one quiet morning when a lookout shouted, "Ship ahoy!"

It was Blackbeard's ship, unmistakable with its dark sails and ominous flag. Henry knew Blackbeard was also after the treasure of Pirate's Cove.

"We must reach the cove before he does," Henry said, his jaw set. "We can't let the treasure fall into the wrong hands."

The race was on. Henry and his crew pushed their ship to its limits, cutting through the waves with renewed purpose. They knew that reaching the treasure first was about more than just the riches; it was about protecting the legacy of Pirate's Cove from the likes of Blackbeard.

And so, with the wind in their sails and determination in their hearts, Henry, Skippy, and their brave crew sailed towards their destiny, unaware of the trials that still awaited them in their quest for the lost treasure.

The race to Pirate's Cove was tense, with Henry's ship and Blackbeard's vessel cutting through the waves, each vying to be the first to reach the legendary treasure. As the cove came into view, a narrow inlet hidden between towering cliffs, Henry knew they were close.

"We're almost there, crew! Man the sails, tighten the ropes!" Henry commanded, his voice ringing with determination.

Skippy fluttered around, squawking encouragement, "Squawk! Almost there, almost there!"

But just as they neared the cove, Blackbeard's ship gained on them, its massive figure casting a shadow over Henry's vessel.

"Arr, you won't beat me to the treasure, young Henry!" bellowed Blackbeard, his voice booming across the water.

Henry glanced back, his resolve unwavering. "We'll see about that, Blackbeard! Full speed ahead!"

With a burst of speed, Henry's ship surged forward, entering the cove just moments before Blackbeard. The crew cheered, but their celebration was short-lived. As they anchored the ship and prepared to disembark, they saw Blackbeard's crew rapidly approaching the shore.

Henry, Skippy, and a few brave crew members hurriedly made their way to the island, map in hand, racing against Blackbeard to find the treasure.

The map led them through dense jungle and up a steep hill. They reached the top, panting and exhausted, only to find Blackbeard and his crew already there, surrounding a large, ancient chest.

"So, you made it first, but it's too late," sneered Blackbeard, his hand on the chest.

Henry stepped forward, his heart pounding. "This treasure doesn't belong to the likes of you, Blackbeard. It belongs to the sea and those who respect it!"

Blackbeard laughed. "Fine words for a youngster, but I'm the one with the chest."

Just then, Skippy swooped down, snatching the key from Blackbeard's hand and flying it over to Henry.

"Quick thinking, Skippy!" Henry exclaimed, catching the key.

In a bold move, Henry opened the chest. A brilliant light shone from within, illuminating their awed faces. The treasure was more magnificent than anyone had imagined, filled with gold, jewels, and ancient artifacts.

Blackbeard lunged forward to grab the treasure, but Henry stood his ground. "This treasure will not be used for greed. We will use it to help others, to make the seas a safer place for everyone."

The standoff was tense, but then, something unexpected happened. Blackbeard, looking into the chest, seemed to soften.

"Perhaps... Perhaps you're right, Henry. Maybe it's time for a change."

In that moment, the rivalry between Henry and Blackbeard dissolved, the realization that true treasure wasn't just gold and jewels, but the courage to do what's right.

Henry smiled, knowing that they had not only found the treasure but also changed the heart of the fiercest pirate on the seas.

With the conflict resolved and the treasure of Pirate's Cove finally in their hands, Henry, Skippy, and their crew, along with a surprisingly cooperative Blackbeard, made their way back to their ships. The air was filled with a new sense of unity and purpose.

As they sailed back to the island, Henry had a plan. "We will use this treasure wisely," he declared. "It will help our island and the seas around us."

Blackbeard, a changed man, nodded in agreement. "Aye, you've shown me there's more to life than plundering. I'll join you in making these waters safe."

The pirates of the island were amazed to see Blackbeard's ship approaching in peace. When Henry and his crew displayed the treasure and shared their story, the islanders were overjoyed.

Henry addressed everyone gathered on the shore. "This treasure is not just ours; it belongs to all who call these waters home. We'll use it to improve our island, help those in need, and protect the sea."

The islanders cheered, moved by Henry's words and actions. Skippy, perched proudly on Henry's shoulder, squawked happily, "Squawk! A true treasure, indeed!"

In the following days, the treasure was used to better the lives of the islanders. They repaired homes, built new ships for safer travels, and even set up a fund to protect the marine life.

Blackbeard, now an ally, helped patrol the waters, ensuring safe passage for all who sailed them. The once-feared pirate had become a guardian of the sea, thanks to Henry's influence.

One evening, as the sun set over the island, Henry and Skippy sat on the beach, watching the waves gently lap the shore.

"You did it, Henry," Skippy said. "You found the treasure and changed the hearts of many."

Henry smiled, looking out at the peaceful sea. "It's not the gold or jewels that make a treasure valuable, Skippy. It's what you do with it that counts. We used it to bring people together, to make a difference. That's the real treasure."

Skippy nodded, his feathers ruffling in the sea breeze. "Squawk! And you're a true leader, Henry. A leader who shares and cares."

As the stars twinkled in the night sky, Henry realized that the greatest adventures didn't just lie in distant lands or hidden treasures, but in the impact one could have on the world and the people around them.

The story of "The Lost Treasure of Pirate's Cove" became a legend, not just for the treasure found, but for the lesson it taught: true leaders share their treasures and successes, making the world a better place for all. And young Henry, with his brave heart and wise soul, became an inspiration to everyone who heard his tale.

In the cozy glow of the Thomas family's living room, under the vigilance of a ticking wall clock and a watchful goldfish named Jupiter, Sam sat sprawled among a sea of crumpled papers and discarded pencils. He was cocooned in concentration, his brows furrowed as he tried to conjure up an idea for his school science fair project.

His younger sister, Luna, clad in her favorite rocket-themed pajamas, peered over his shoulder with curious eyes. "What's that supposed to be?" she asked, poking at a scribble that vaguely resembled a flying saucer.

Sam sighed, his shoulder slumping slightly. "It was supposed to be a hovercraft, but it just looks like a deflated pancake." He crumpled another sheet of paper, the idea joining the graveyard of attempts around him.

"Don't give up, Sam," Luna chirped, picking up a paper airplane and sending it gliding across the room. "You'll think of something zoomy and zappy."

Just then, their mom called out, "Kids! Time to get ready for bed. Don't forget, we're stargazing tonight!"

Eyes lighting up, Sam pushed the papers aside. "That's it! What if I build a space station?"

Luna's grin was wide as the Milky Way. "That sounds out of this world!"

Up on the hill behind their house, the night sky stretched like a black canvas dotted with twinkling cosmic paint. Sam lay next to Luna, their gazes locked on the stars above.

"This will be the best project ever," Sam whispered, his mind racing with possibilities. "A space station that—"

"Gets power from the sun?" Luna finished excitedly. "Solar panels!"

"Yes!" Sam sat up, animated by the vision. "Sam's Solar Space Station, powered entirely by the sun!"

Back in the classroom the following day, Mr. Clarke was concluding his lecture about the importance of renewable energy. Sam's hand shot up like a rocket.

"Mr. Clarke! Can a space station really be powered by the sun?"

The corner of Mr. Clarke's mouth curled into a smile. "Absolutely, Sam. In fact, solar energy is very efficient in space. Do you have an idea for our science fair?"

"I do." Sam straightened proudly. "I'm going to build a solar-powered space station model!"

Mr. Clarke nodded approvingly. "That's an ambitious project, Sam. But remember, science isn't just about individual success; it's about sharing ideas and working together."

At recess, Sam recounted his plan to his classmates, his hands weaving through the air as he described the solar space station.

"You think you can pull it off?" asked one of the skeptical kids, kicking a pebble.

Sam hesitated, the seed of doubt threatening his newfound resolve. Just then, Luna skipped over. "Of course he can! And I'll help him!"

Sam's confidence returned, bolstered by his sister's unwavering belief. "We're going to make it work. Just you wait and see!" Luna beamed at her brother's side, ready to embark on their celestial project together.

The weeks leading up to the fair were a blizzard of activity. Sam and Luna converted their garage into a makeshift workshop, complete with spare parts and tools that they gathered from around the house. They worked tirelessly, with Luna diving into piles of wires and circuit boards, and Sam sketching and constructing the frame of the space station.

"Do you think we'll have enough time?" Sam asked one afternoon, while they were taking a short break and munching on cheese sandwiches.

"We have to," Luna replied with determination. "We just need to break this project down, step by step."

Day by day, the structure began to take shape. Sam carefully cut and assembled the support beams, while Luna tinkered with the mini solar panels. Their synergy was evident, with Sam's vision guiding them and Luna's technical know-how bringing it to life.

One evening, as the sun dipped below the horizon, Mr. Clarke stopped by their workshop upon hearing of their ambitious endeavor.

"How's the space station coming along, young scientists?" he asked, peering at the intertwining maze of beams and panels.

"It's going," Luna said. "But we're trying to figure out how to make the solar cells more efficient."

Mr. Clarke nodded and offered a few tips, explaining how they could optimize the angle of the panels. As he left, he turned back with a smile. "Remember, it's not just about the project itself. It's about the problem-solving skills you're developing."

His words stuck with Sam as they progressed. They managed to recalibrate the solar cells, and suddenly the space station's heart began to glow with life, its LED lights powered solely by the panels.

As the science fair approached, they performed test after test, ensuring that all systems were operational. The living room had become mission control, with countdowns and checklists plastering the walls.

However, with their focus on functionality, aesthetics had taken a backseat. Sam looked at the station, its appearance not as polished or sleek as he had imagined.

"Do you think it looks okay?" he asked Luna.

"It looks like something a real space engineer would make," Luna assured him with a confident nod. "It might not be shiny, but it works, and that's what counts. Plus, it's eco-friendly!"

Finally, the last school bell before the fair rang, and a mixture of excitement and nervousness filled the air.

"We've done everything we could," Sam said as they prepared to bring their creation to school. "Now it's just a matter of showing everyone else." Luna slipped her hand into Sam's as they wheeled the model towards school, the LED lights flickering like distant stars against the dusk sky, and their anticipation as vast as space itself.

The sun had barely peeked over the horizon when Sam and Luna arrived at the school gymnasium, their eyes heavy with the last night's work and minds buzzing with anticipation. Together, they wheeled in their creation, covered with a large gray tarp to keep it a surprise.

As they set up their booth, carefully removing the tarp, a collective gasp swept through the early crowd of students and teachers. The space station stood proudly, a beacon of cardboard, foil, and blinking lights powered by the neatly installed solar panels.

"What an incredible project!" exclaimed Mrs. Bennett, the school librarian, her glasses perched low on her nose as she examined the station.

Sam beamed with pride, and Luna, her hands on her hips, nodded in agreement. But as more students poured in, showcasing flashy projects with bright colors and high-tech devices, Sam's smile faltered.

"Look at all this cool stuff, Luna," he whispered. "They're so... professional."

Luna squeezed his hand. "But none of them are solar powered. Ours is unique, and that's what matters."

Before long, the gym was bustling with excitement, and the fair officially began. Sam and Luna were kept busy answering questions and demonstrating their solar panels. Sam found himself growing more and more confident with each explanation and glowing comment.

But then disaster struck. In the midst of a demonstration, the main power line snagged, ripping a panel off the side of the station. The LED lights flickered and died. Chatter around them ceased as everyone turned to see the source of the commotion.

Sam's heart plummeted. All the hard work, all the restless nights, seemed to unravel before his eyes.

"It's okay, Sam," Luna said, though her eyes were wide with panic. "We can fix this."

Sam kneeled by the broken part, hands trembling slightly as he considered their options. "We need to reroute the power. Can you patch a secondary line to bypass this panel?"

Luna nodded, scrambling to the task. Sam could feel the eyes of the fair's attendees on them, but he focused solely on the wires in front of him.

As Luna pulled a set of wires from her pocket, Sam expertly twisted them together, connecting the circuits. With a deep breath, he pressed the makeshift switch.

The lights flickered, waned, then shone brightly once more. A cheer erupted from around them, and Sam could barely believe it. They had done it. Under pressure, with their backs against the wall, they had persevered.

The rest of the fair was a blur as Sam and Luna floated through on a cloud of relief and pride. When it came time for the judges to make their rounds, Sam found himself less concerned with their verdict. They had proven to themselves what they could achieve, and that was worth more than any ribbon or prize.

As the judges moved through the gymnasium, their clipboards tucked under their arms, Sam and Luna stood by their solar space station, a trove of patched-together wires hidden by the shadow of the display. The fair had been a whirlwind, but as the end drew near, a hush descended upon the room, every student waiting with bated breath for the results.

The judges paused at each entry, scribbling notes and murmuring among themselves. Eventually, they stopped in front of Sam and Luna's booth. The children looked up with hopeful eyes as the judges examined their project, the warmth of the gymnasium making the air feel thick with anticipation.

"Tell us about your project," prompted one judge, a kind-faced woman with a sharp gaze that seemed to take in every detail.

Sam cleared his throat. "This is Sam's Solar Space Station. It's powered entirely by these solar panels, which convert sunlight into energy for all the onboard systems."

"And we made sure to use recycled and eco-friendly materials where we could," Luna added, pointing out the solar cell array.

One of the judges leaned closer, inspecting the wiring. "I see you had a bit of a setback earlier. How did you manage to fix it?"

Luna smiled. "A space mission doesn't always go perfectly—you have to adapt. So we created a bypass for the power flow, and now it's as good as new!"

The judges nodded in approval, making a final tick on their clipboards, before moving on to the next exhibit.

As the afternoon waned, the moment of truth finally arrived. The head judge stepped forward with the list of winners. Sam felt Luna's hand grip his tightly.

"We've seen some remarkable projects today," the head judge began. "But we were particularly impressed by one that not only displayed a keen understanding of science but also was built on the principles of sustainability and resilience."

Sam's heart thudded in his chest, but he found himself thinking, win or lose, we did something amazing.

The head judge continued, "The award for 'Best Sustainable Project' goes to Sam's Solar Space Station!"

A round of applause filled the gym, and Luna leapt into Sam's arms, laughing. They wove their way up to the front, accepting the certificate with wide grins.

As they returned to their station, Mr. Clarke approached, his eyes twinkling with pride. "You both showed great innovation and teamwork today," he said. "And remember, the true value lies not in the award but in the lessons you've learned and the obstacles you've overcome together."

Sam nodded, a sense of accomplishment swelling in his chest. "We did it together, Luna. And we learned that no challenge is too great when we work as a team."

The sun was setting as they eventually packed up their space station. The gym was empty, the excitement had faded, but Sam and Luna left hand in hand, their award in the other, knowing that the journey of learning and sharing didn't end there—it was just the beginning.

The Valiant Voyager cut through the sparkling blue sea with grace and vigor, its sails billowing like the wings of an albatross in flight. Captain Chris stood at the helm with a firm grip on the wheel, his eager eyes scanning the horizon. The sun was warm on his face, and the salty breeze tousled his auburn hair.

"Avast, Ali! Make fast the topsail! We don't want to be caught off our guard," Captain Chris called out, his voice carrying above the gentle lap of waves against the hull.

"Aye, Captain!" Ali replied with a grin, scampering up the ropes with the agility of a cat. His laughter rang out as he secured the canvas with swift, precise knots.

Below deck, Zoe emerged, her hands full of maps scattered with X's and dotted lines. She squinted up at the bright sky and then at the compass in her hand, her brow furrowed in concentration.

"The winds are in our favor today!" Zoe shouted up to the two, her voice brimming with excitement. "The uncharted isles should be just over the next sunrise if the sea remains our friend."

Captain Chris met her enthusiasm with a hearty laugh. "You hear that, crew? Adventure awaits, but only if Zoe here keeps us on course," he teased, winking at his dear friend.

Their laughter mingled with the call of seagulls and the rhythmic creaking of the ship. Spirits were high as they anticipated the wonders they would find at their destination.

But as the day waned into a gold-streaked evening, a queer hush fell over The Valiant Voyager. The wind picked up, carrying with it a sudden chill that seemed out of place under the still-bright summer sun.

Captain Chris's jovial expression turned serious. "Ali, Zoe, come close," he commanded, his voice now a measured calm that masked the surge of adrenaline he felt. "A squall is nigh. I can feel it in the marrow of the ship."

And indeed, as if on cue, a darkness gathered in the distance, an ominous ink blot spreading rapidly across the previously clear sky. The wind escalated to a howl, and the first wave came crashing over The Valiant Voyager's bow, drenching them all in a cool spray.

Without panic, Captain Chris took action. "Prepare the sails, reef the main! And Zoe, secure anything loose below! We must show this storm the mettle of our crew!"

Ali, though soaked and bracing against the vessel's sway, nodded and set to work. "Aye, aye, Captain! I've not met a storm that can best me yet!"

Zoe dashed to obey, her voice firm, yet tinged with the thrill of the impending challenge. "I'll see that we lose not a single scroll!"

The seas grew more menacing with every passing minute, and just when they thought they might have a grasp on the tempest's fury, a monstrous wave loomed over them, and with a resounding crack, the ship's wheel snapped off in Captain Chris's hands.

A collective gasp escaped the crew as Captain Chris examined the broken wheel, the heart of The Valiant Voyager now in pieces. With no time to dwell on their misfortune, Captain Chris's mind raced for a solution.

"Ali, Zoe, to me!" he bellowed, his voice slicing through the uproar of wind and waves. "We're not just sailors—we're survivors. We'll steer her true without a wheel if we must!"

Ali and Zoe, drenched from head to toe but undeterred, rushed to his side, their eyes wide but determined.

"What's the plan, Captain?" Ali shouted, grappling onto the rail to steady himself.

Zoe, her hands tightly clutching a coil of rope, added, "We need your orders!"

"We'll fashion a makeshift tiller," Captain Chris said, his mind already envisioning the contraption. "We'll need the spare spars and as much rope as we can spare. Ali, gather the material. Zoe, help me tie off what's left of the rudder!"

They sprang into action. The ship wrestled with the savage sea, each wave a brute force that threatened to claim The Valiant Voyager as its own. Ali returned with the spars, the wood clattering against the deck as he dropped it to join his efforts with Zoe.

"Together now!" Captain Chris encouraged over the roar. "Tie it off as if your lives depended on it, because they do!"

Their fingers worked swiftly, securing the spars to the remnants of the rudder, binding and knotting with a sailor's expertise. The once disciplined movement of The Valiant Voyager had now become a desperate struggle against the tempest's might.

Zoe glanced up at Captain Chris, worry etched on her features. "This storm is like none we've seen before!"

Captain Chris, though gripping the makeshift tiller, maintained a calm exterior. "Aye, but we've seen many a storm, and we'll see many more. This is but another story to tell!"

Suddenly, a towering wall of water surged from the deep, barreling toward them with a fury that turned day to night.

"Hold fast!" The captain's command was just audible over the impending crash.

They braced themselves, and the wave struck with a force that shook The Valiant Voyager to its core. When the chaos subsided, the crew found themselves still afloat, still together, their creation miraculously intact.

Another challenge loomed as they spotted dangerous rock formations ahead, hidden by the surging waters that now enshrouded their path. Captain Chris's heart pounded—a collision would mean the end of their voyage, perhaps the end of all their tales.

Zoe's voice broke through the panic, "We can't let the rocks take us, Captain! We must steer clear!"

"You've the heart of a lion, Zoe! Ali, with me—we'll navigate these waters like the legends of old!"

The makeshift tiller held, Ali and Captain Chris strained at the wood, veins standing out on their foreheads as they fought to avoid the jagged teeth rising from the depths. Each crew member's resolve stood as strong as the iron bonds of the ship, their determination the beacon that would lead them through the storm's dark veil.

The ship lurched and groaned under the force of nature's wrath as Captain Chris and Ali held fast to the spar, guiding The Valiant Voyager with sheer will and muscle. Zoe kept a steady watch ahead, her keen eyes searching through the rain and spray for the next threat.

"There!" Zoe pointed to a gap between the rocks. "Head starboard, Captain! It's our only chance!"

Captain Chris nodded. "Ali, on my count! One, two, three—push!"

Using the spar as a lever, they angled the ship's course just as another wave bore down upon them. The deck tilted perilously, the crew clinging on for dear life, their knuckles white with tension.

"We're making it through!" Ali cheered, despite the howling wind that tried to steal away his words.

But the ocean was not yet finished with its assault. A colossal wave rose, shadowing the ship like a behemoth from the deep, ready to swallow them whole.

"This is it, crew!" Captain Chris called out, his eyes alight with an unquenchable fire of leadership. "Hold true!"

They braced themselves, the ship pitching wildly as the wave collided. Water crashed over them, blinding and choking. They coughed and sputtered, struggling to find footing, but when the deluge receded, to their astonishment, they were intact, the rocks now behind them.

Zoe let out a triumphant whoop. "By the stars, we've done it!"

Captain Chris exhaled a long breath, allowing himself a fleeting smile. "Not yet. We've not collapsed the teeth of the tempest just so it can swallow us whole. Stay vigilant."

The storm raged on, but with each maneuver and each command barked by Captain Chris, The Valiant Voyager persevered. The crew's spirits rallied, fueled by the indomitable courage of their captain.

Then, amidst the cacophony of the gale, the sea began to change. The dark clouds thinned, allowing brief glimpses of a star-studded sky. The wind lost its biting edge, now racing and sweeping about them with less fury.

As the tempest's force waned, Captain Chris stood firm, his eyes reflecting a sky slowly reclaiming its serenity.

"Weathered the storm, we have," he said, a mix of relief and pride in his voice.
Ali slapped Captain Chris on the back. "You've steered us true, Captain! You've steered us right through the heart of it!"

Zoe nodded, her smile radiant. "A night to remember, and a tale to be told! The Courageous Captain and his dauntless crew!"

They stood together on the drenched deck of The Valiant Voyager, no longer just a crew, but a family forged through the fury of the sea. They had faced the storm's might and come out braver and closer than ever before. The ship carried not only the weight of its cargo but the unshakeable spirit of its crew, bonded by the trial of the stormy sea.

As dawn broke, the last of the dark clouds parted, revealing a sunrise of gold and pink streaks painting the calm seascape. The Valiant Voyager, scarred but undefeated by the night's trials, sailed towards a newfound peace. Captain Chris, Ali, and Zoe took in the sight of a lush, inviting island on the horizon.

"Land ho!" Ali shouted with a laugh, his voice filled with wonder and exhaustion.

Zoe leaned on the railing, her eyes softening at the sight of safety. "It looks like paradise after a night like that."

Captain Chris joined his two friends at the ship's side. "You did well. Not many could say they've stared down a storm's wrath and lived to see the morning. It's your hearts and your will that saw us through."

Zoe beamed, basking in the light of the new day and their captain's praise. "We did what we had to do, Captain. We are The Valiant Voyager's crew, after all."

Captain Chris nodded with approval as they dropped anchor near the verdant shores of the island. "The storm has taught us much. We fought fear and uncertainty together and emerged stronger. True leadership, it seems, is less about giving orders and more about standing shoulder to shoulder with your crew."

Ali wrapped his arm around the captain's shoulder. "We'd follow you through any storm, Captain Chris. You showed us that courage isn't just about facing danger, but about facing it with others, lifting them up when they falter."

Captain Chris smiled warmly, grateful for the trust and friendship that had been their true north throughout the ordeal. "And every one of us, no matter how stormy the sea, has the power to lead, to inspire, and to protect one another."

The crew set about repairing their dear ship, their movements synchronized, their songs of labor mingling with the calls of tropical birds from the island. They retold their tales of the night with laughs and gasps, each one contributing a verse to their shared saga.

As the sun climbed higher, Captain Chris took up his quill and began to etch their adventure into the ship's log. The words flowed freely, a testament to their indomitable will. "Through the courage of every crew member, The Valiant Voyager faced the stormy sea and prevailed."

Days would pass, and The Valiant Voyager would set sail again, but the memory of that stormy night would forever be etched in their hearts. They had learned that the true measure of a captain isn't in the commands issued, but in the unity forged in the eye of the storm, a unity that turns a crew into heroes of their own legendary tale.

Max zipped up his jacket, a puff of breath visible in the crisp mountain air, as he stepped back to admire their campsite. The tents stood in a small clearing, flanked by towering pines and the gentle babble of a nearby stream. The smell of pine mixed with the scent of a freshly lit campfire, completing the symphony of nature that surrounded Max and his friends, Sara and Liam.

"Perfect spot, right?" Max said, beaming with pride. Sara, her hair tied back in a practical ponytail, nodded in agreement.

"It's beautiful, and we're close enough to the stream for water," Sara praised, laying out her neatly packed gear. Liam, ever cautious, cast a wary glance at the surrounding woods.

"Yeah, but aren't there bears around here?" Liam's voice carried a tremble that he couldn't quite hide. Max laughed and clapped him on the back.

"Don't worry, I read up on it. We're perfectly safe if we follow the right precautions!" Max reassured him, as Sara chimed in.

"And we'll keep our food stored away. Right, Max?" she interjected with a knowing look.

"Right, Sara. Storage bins, remember?" Max grinned at her attention to detail.

As evening settled, the three friends huddled around their fledgling campfire, the mountain's chill kept at bay by the warm glow of the flames. Their laughter filled the air until a deep voice cut through their merriment.

"Evening, young explorers," a park ranger greeted, tipping his wide-brimmed hat. The kids greeted him excitedly, asking questions about the wildlife and trails.

"How about a story about the mountains?" Sara asked with a curious tilt of her head. The ranger's eyes twinkled with the opportunity, and he leaned in.

"Have you heard of Echo Cave?"

Max shook his head, his interest piqued. "No, what's that?"

"A cave somewhere in these mountains," the ranger said with a mysterious undertone, "It's said that deep within its chambers, the echoes can tell you secrets about the mountains that no one else knows."

"Wow," Liam whispered, "But... has anyone ever found it?"

The ranger stroked his chin. "Many have searched, but few have found it. It's tricky, the path isn't straightforward, and you need the heart of an adventurer to navigate it."

Max's eyes sparkled in the firelight. This was it—the adventure he had been craving. He knew, in that instant, what they'd be doing tomorrow.

"We're going to find that cave," Max announced resolutely, standing up with determination.

Sara nodded, excitement replacing her cautious demeanor. "We can do it if we stick together."

Liam hesitated but looking at his friends' excited faces, he mustered a smile. "Alright, but we're planning this out first. No running headfirst into it, okay?"

"Agree!" Max exclaimed, "We'll be like the explorers of old, discovering new lands!"

And so, under the blanket of stars, they plotted their grand quest, not knowing what lay ahead, but certain that together they could face anything the mountain had to offer.

The dawn crept over the mountains as Max, Sara, and Liam readied themselves with supplies for their expedition to Echo Cave. Max checked the straps on his backpack, making sure everything was secure. Sara unfolded a rough map a kind old camper had sketched for them, her eyes scanning the lines and curves that marked the terrain.

"This should take us close to where the cave is supposed to be," she said with confidence.

"Let's make sure our flashlights are working," Liam suggested, clicking his on and off. "Don't want any surprises in the dark."

The morning air was filled with the sounds of chirping birds and rustling leaves as they set off, a trail of boot prints behind them, weaving through the forest. They encountered a stream with water so clear, the stones at the bottom sparkled like jewels. They jumped from rock to rock, laughing when a splash sent cold droplets onto their skin.

"So far, so good, guys!" Max exclaimed with a grin.

A couple of hours into their journey, the dense canopy above cast the forest into deeper shades of green and the underbrush grew thicker. They used a stick to push aside the ferns and low-hanging branches that blocked their path.

Sara paused, holding up a hand. "Listen," she whispered, and the three stood still, the silence around them humming with anticipation. In the distance, a faint, repetitive sound reached their ears.

"Is that... an echo?" Liam asked, excitement pushing aside his earlier anxieties.

They followed the sound until they stood before a rugged cliff, the entrance of Echo Cave looming like a giant's mouth, the echoes dancing out from the darkness within.

"This is it!" Max said, his voice echoing into the cave, a symphony of whispers returned to them.

The cave welcomed them with a cool breath as they stepped tentatively inside. The beams of their flashlights darted around, illuminating ancient walls worn smooth by time. Their voices bounced back to them, a chorus of their own making.

Along the caverns, they marveled at the stalactites clinging to the ceiling, creating an otherworldly landscape. They walked deeper into the cave, the light from the entrance fading behind them.

Sara pointed to a series of faded drawings on the wall, "Look! These could be centuries old!"

Max touched the cool rock, "Imagine who might have used this cave before us?"

They ventured further, deep conversation illuminating their path with thoughts of the past, but as they rounded another bend, they were confronted by a sight that brought them to a sudden stop.

A collapse had blocked the path ahead, rocks and debris forming an impassable wall. Liam gulped, "We can't go any further."

But Max moved closer, inspecting the pile. "There has to be another way," he mused, his flashlight scanning for openings.

Then, in a stroke of luck, a faint draft brushed his face. "Feel this!" he urged. "Air's coming through!" They cleared smaller stones with urgency, revealing the faint outline of a passage.

"Our next move," Max proclaimed, looking at Sara and Liam, eyes alight with adventure, "is through there!"

The trio squeezed one by one through the crevice, the sound of shifting rocks under their hands and knees echoing through the tight space. As they emerged, they found themselves in a smaller chamber, the passage continuing into deeper darkness ahead.

"This has to be the right way," whispered Max, leading the way with his flashlight beaming a path forward.

The air grew cooler as they progressed, the distant sound of dripping water playing rhythm to their careful steps. They encountered natural obstacles, from slippery stones to narrow ledges that demanded each ounce of their focus and bravery.

Sara kept up the rear, her voice steady, "Keep an eye on the ground, guys. No telling what's under all this dirt."

Liam nodded, gripping his flashlight like a lifeline. Every shadow seemed to dance, making his imagination run wild with thoughts of hidden creatures watching from the gloom. "How much farther do you think it is?" he asked, trying to keep the waver out of his voice.

Max consulted the fading scribbles on their makeshift map. "We can't be that far now. The ranger said it was deep within the mountain."

They edged along a precipitous drop, the void yawning beside them hungrily. Max took the lead, offering a hand to steady Liam. Sara followed, her eyes carefully measuring each foothold. Just as they cleared the drop, they stopped, nearly catching their breaths in their throats.

In front of them stood a giant boulder lodged between the floor and the ceiling, blocking their way. The echoing voices seemed to bounce off it mockingly.

"There's no way around it," Liam said, his disappointment heavy as the stone blocking their path.

Max approached the boulder, laying a hand on its cold surface. The air around it felt different — fresher, somehow. He pressed his ear to the stone, listening. There was a sound coming from the other side, a faint but distinctive murmur. "Guys, there's something behind this! Can you hear it?" he called out excitedly.

Sara joined him, her face lighting up as she caught the noise. "It's like the cave is alive."

Liam moved closer, curiosity replacing his fear. "But... how do we get past it?"

Max examined the boulder closely, his eyes tracing its edges, searching for any clue. "That's it!" he shouted. There was a thin gap at the base of the rock, just enough space to show there was more cave beyond it.

Energized with newfound determination, they started to dig with their hands, pulling away the loose earth. As they worked, the gap started to widen, the fresh air seeping through beckoning them to the secrets that lay just beyond their reach.

"Come on, we're almost there! We can't give up now!" Max encouraged, his voice echoing into the widening aperture.

Sweat dripped down their foreheads, mixing with the dirt on their faces. They worked with a united rhythm, until, with one last heave from all three, the boulder shifted, groaning a protest as it moved just enough to create a passage.

With a collective breath of anticipation and thrill, they took turns slipping past the boulder. What lay before them was beyond anything they could have imagined, a space so vast and extraordinary that for a moment, they could only stand and stare in wonder.

The chamber that opened up before them was a cathedral of nature, its walls glittering with crystals that refracted their flashlight beams into a kaleidoscope of colors. Stalagmites rose from the ground like statues, and the echoes that once seemed whispers were now a choir of ancient songs.

"Whoa..." Liam's voice was a hushed exclamation, his earlier fears forgotten in the face of such splendor.

"We found it," Sara breathed out, a mixture of awe and pride in her voice, "the heart of Echo Cave."

Max stepped forward, his light sweeping across the shimmering formations. "And we're the first to see it like this... probably in forever!"

As they ventured deeper into the grotto, every step was careful, reverent. They didn't speak much; there was no need. The cave spoke for them, its echoes a constant companion. They found a small pool of water, so clear that the bottom seemed to shine with its own light, the stones like jewels.

They knew they couldn't stay forever, though every inch of the cavern begged to be explored.

"We should mark our path," Liam suggested. "So we can show everyone where we've been."

With small cairns of stones, they marked their journey through the grotto, ensuring the path home was clear. They realized, as they assembled the last one, that night must be falling outside. It was time to head back.

As they retraced their steps, with everyone lending a hand to carefully move past the boulder, a feeling of accomplishment filled the air. They moved through the passages they'd conquered, and each step out of the cave felt lighter, freer.

At the mouth of Echo Cave, the fading light of the sun greeted them, and they stepped out to see the stars twinkling above them. They understood then that courage wasn't just about facing the unknown, but also knowing when it was time to return and share the treasures you'd found.

"That was the most incredible thing I've ever seen," Liam exclaimed, a newfound spark in his eyes.

Sara nodded, "It was amazing... and we did it together."

Max looked at his friends, pride swelling in his chest. "We were brave, and we were curious, and look what we found!"

"And we supported each other," Sara added, her hand on Liam's shoulder, "even when one of us was scared. That's what friends do."

Liam smiled, a broad, true smile. "Yeah. Adventure is great, but it's nothing if you can't tell the story to someone afterward."

With the evening chill settling around them, they made their way back to the campsite, their hearts full of memories, their minds buzzing with tales of bravery, friendship, and the sparkling wonders of Echo Cave.

That night, as they recounted their journey to the other campers, the sky seemed to sparkle a little brighter above them, the stars like the crystals of Echo Cave, winking in approval of the brave explorers' return.

In the heart of the magnificent kingdom of Greenwood, with verdant meadows stretching to the horizon and rivers that glinted like spun silver under the sun, stood a castle as grand as the legends surrounding it. This was the home of King Arthur, whose youthful enthusiasm was matched only by his fervent wish to be a wise and fair ruler to his people.

On this particular day, the castle was abuzz with excitement. Villagers in colorful garb filled the courtyards, knights polished their armor until it sparkled, and minstrels practiced their sweetest ballads. Inside the great hall, the young King Arthur, with his round table not far, was holding court.

"Merlin," King Arthur said, turning towards his sage advisor who was thumbing through an ancient tome, "The people seem to carry joy in their steps today. The air is filled with merriment."

Merlin looked up from his book, peering over the rims of his half-moon spectacles, and smiled. "Indeed, Sire. Today, Greenwood thrives. Your heart is generous, and your subjects feel the warmth of your goodwill."

Just then, Guinevere burst through the doors, her cheeks flushed with the wind's kiss. "Arthur," she called. "The meadows are alive with laughter! The jousters are as eager as spring colts! Come, you must see for yourself!"

Arthur's eyes shone with delight. "I shall join you shortly, but first, we must finish the day's matters of the crown."

As the affairs of the kingdom were addressed, an unusual shadow passed over the sun, casting an eerie gloom over the hall. A deep rumble echoed through the stones, and whispers turned to gasps as all eyes turned to the source.

In strode a messenger, bowing low before the king. "Great Arthur," his voice shook, "A challenge has been issued. The Great Dragon of the North seeks an audience with you. It threatens eternal winter upon Greenwood unless the wisest ruler can answer its riddles."

The court erupted in murmurs, but Arthur held up a hand for silence. "We shall not succumb to fear," he said firmly. "As king, I will face this dragon and its challenge. Greenwood shall not fall into an icy slumber!"

Merlin approached, a frown carving deep lines in his brow. "My Lord, wisdom is often found in patience. It may be prudent to consider the dragon's challenge carefully."

Arthur nodded. "And we shall, dear Merlin. We begin at dawn. I will consult with you and Guinevere. Together, we shall solve these riddles for the sake of our kingdom."

Guinevere stepped forward, her eyes resolute. "You won't face this alone, Arthur. With the courage and kinship of your friends, and the guidance of Merlin's wisdom, we will meet this dragon and safeguard our home."

The hall, filled with tension moments before, now radiated with a quiet strength—a kingdom united, with a youthful king at its helm, ready to rise to any challenge.

As dawn's first light kissed the dew-drenched cobblestones of Greenwood, King Arthur, Merlin, and Guinevere set forth on their grand quest. The kingdom they left behind was a portrait of quiet courage, its people watching their sovereign disappear into the veil of morning mist with a collective, hopeful breath.

Their journey first led them through emerald woods, where sunlight dappled the ground through the leaves and birdsong filled the air.

Merlin, whose eyes missed little, would often pause to pluck herbs or study some curious beetle's path. "Tell me, Arthur," he said as he examined the veins of a leaf, "What do you believe constitutes true wisdom?"

Arthur thought for a moment before replying, "To rule well and to lead my people to prosperity."

"Not a leaf, not a stone, not a creature in this forest exists solely for itself, young king," Merlin replied cryptically. "Remember that wisdom is the tapestry woven from the countless threads of experiences shared."

Pondering Merlin's words, Arthur hardly noticed when they emerged at the edge of a bustling village, where a jester spun riddles and tales for a circle of captivated children.

"What has a heart that does not beat?" called out the jester, a glint in his eye as he spotted the royal travelers.

Without hesitation, Guinevere responded, "A stone!"

The jester bowed playfully. "Ah, a mind swift as the river's flow! What say you, King of Greenwood, will you answer my next?"

Arthur agreed, and the jester posed, "What can run but never walks, has a mouth but never talks?"

"Ah, that would be a river," Arthur replied, the answer coming to him as he recalled the streams they had crossed at daybreak.

The jester clapped with delight. "Well answered indeed. May your quest be fruitful as your wit is keen!"

Leaving the village with the jester's laughter still in their ears, the party delved deeper into lands unknown. They crossed paths with a wise woman drawing water from a well, her gaze knowing and deep.

"Sire," she called to Arthur. "The weight of a crown is heavy, and the path of wisdom is steep."

She reached towards the water, cupping some in her hand. "What is as light as a feather, but even the mightiest of kings cannot hold it for long?"

Merlin and Guinevere turned to Arthur, who was suddenly quiet, his brow furrowed in thought. "It is breath," he finally said, the answer coming to him, as surely as the rise and fall of his own chest.

The wise woman nodded, her smile like the breaking of dawn upon the fields. "You are learning, young sovereign. Wisdom oft lies in the simplest of things."

With each encounter, each challenge met, Arthur felt the roots of understanding spread deeper within his soul. Yet, the dragon's riddles that waited at the journey's end were sure to be woven from far more complex yarns. The young king found himself wondering if he would be ready to rise to the dragon's cryptic challenges.

The mountain loomed before them, capped with snow that reflected the sky's azure canvas. The path that wound toward its peak was strewn with rocks, and the air grew thin and cool as King Arthur and his companions ascended.

"Each step forward is a triumph in itself, Your Majesty," Merlin said, his breath forming clouds in the chill air.

"We cannot falter now," Guinevere added, her words an anchor in the mountain's daunting presence.

Finally, they stood at the mountain's summit, where a vast plateau stretched out before them. There, coiled amidst steaming vents and shards of ice, lay the Great Dragon of the North. Its scales shimmered like jewels over a body as long as the river that ran through Greenwood. It opened its eyes, and they glowed with a brilliance unmatched by any crown jewel Arthur had ever seen.

"Come, King of Greenwood," the Dragon's voice rumbled, deep and ageless. "Answer my riddles three, or an endless winter shall your kingdom see."

Arthur stepped forward. "Speak your riddles, mighty dragon. I am ready."

The Dragon's tail thudded upon the ground, forcing all to steady themselves. "First riddle: I touch the earth, I touch the sky. But if I touch you, you will surely die."

Arthur's heart raced, but he drew a deep breath and looked to the skies above, then to the ground below before his gaze settled on the Dragon's snout. "You are the clouds," he declared. "You can touch the sky and the mountains, but should you touch a man, he would perish at such heights."

A low rumble of approval echoed, the Dragon nodding its great head. "Well met, young king. Now, the second riddle: I am not alive, but I grow; I do not have lungs, but I need air; I do not have a mouth, but water kills me."

Arthur looked to Merlin, who merely nodded, encouraging the young king to trust his instincts. Casting his thoughts wide, Arthur recalled the laughter of villagers, the sights of the bustling markets, and the stories of the countryside. A spark of realization flickered within.

"You are fire," Arthur announced. The dragon's scales gleamed brighter, casting prismatic light on the icy plateau.

"Indeed," the Dragon approved. "Now, the final riddle, the one upon which your fate hangs: I am light as a feather, yet even the strongest cannot hold me for much longer than a minute. What am I?"

Arthur's mind reeled. The confidence he had felt was now replaced by a burgeoning sense of doubt. He struggled to focus, his thoughts scattering like leaves in the wind.

Merlin's voice whispered on the breeze, "Look within, Arthur. Remember the wise woman's words."

Guinevere's eyes were steady and calm, her trust in him unwavering. Suddenly, it dawned on him – the answer lay not in the riddle itself but in the sum of all he had learned on this quest.

With newfound clarity, Arthur spoke. "You are breath, the very essence of life and the whisper of wisdom."

A sizzling sound filled the air, like fire meeting ice, and then, silence. The Dragon's eyes dimmed with a gentle light, a silent acknowledgment of the wisdom King Arthur had found. With the final riddle solved, the threat of eternal winter faded, and the true trial of Arthur's leadership had reached its zenith. The wisdom of a king was not bestowed; it was forged in the crucible of challenges met and lessons learned.

The Great Dragon relaxed its coiled form, and the ice that encased the mountain peak began to melt away, cascading down the slopes in a symphony of bubbling streams. The warmth of spring returned to the air, and the great beast unfolded its wings, which blotted out the sun for a moment before settling again.

"You have proven yourself, King Arthur," the Dragon spoke, its voice now carrying a note of reverence. "Your heart and judgment are true. Greenwood is blessed to have a ruler who seeks wisdom with such a fervent spirit."

Arthur stood tall, a sense of pride swelling within him, but it was a pride tempered with humility. "Your riddles have taught me much, Great Dragon. They were not just challenges to be bested, but lessons I will carry with me as long as I sit on the throne."

The Dragon nodded. "A kingdom's strength lies not in its armies or treasures, but in the wisdom of its ruler. Go forth, King Arthur, and lead with the insight you have gained this day."

As the Dragon took to the skies, its form becoming but a speck against the sun, Merlin, Guinevere, and Arthur began their descent. As they walked, Arthur reflected on their journey and the kindness, bravery, and intelligence of his people that had guided him to answer the riddles.

"My friends," Arthur said, "I once thought that to be a wise king, I needed only to be brave and just. But wisdom is the compass that guides those virtues. It is the light that turns a hopeful path into a sure one."

Merlin inclined his head. "Indeed, Sire. But remember, wisdom is not a destination but a journey—one that does not end."

"And it is a journey we will walk together," Guinevere added, beaming at them both. "For even the wisest need friends by their side."

They returned to Greenwood to cheers and relief. The kingdom celebrated, but Arthur knew the festivities heralded not just the end of the dragon's challenge but the beginning of his own journey toward ever-greater wisdom.

In the days that followed, Arthur applied his new understanding to his rule. He listened more and spoke less. He observed the world with keener eyes and considered his decisions with a clearer mind. And most importantly, he turned to his advisors and his people, drawing on their collective wisdom to forge a brighter future for all.

As the young king stood at his castle balcony, looking over the kingdom that thrived under his care, he realized that wisdom wasn't just about intelligence or knowledge but about the courage to ask questions, the willingness to learn from others, and the humble acceptance of ever-unfolding truths.

And so, the king who had once sought wisdom now lived it every day, and Greenwood prospered as never before under the reign of the Wise King Arthur, whose greatest strength lay in the wisdom that warmed his heart and guided his hand.

The autumn leaves danced like sparks from a campfire as the sun dipped below the rooftops of Maple Street. Laughter echoed through the crisp fall air, where a group of neighborhood kids had gathered under the old tree in the park. Its branches were a sturdy testament to the many secrets and dreams they held within their woody embrace.

"Look at this one!" Leo exclaimed, holding up a particularly bright maple leaf. It was as red as the evening sun, its edges tinged with gold.

Mia glanced up from her sketchpad, her brown eyes reflecting the leaf's fiery colors. "It's like a piece of the sun decided to visit us," she said with a smile, promptly reaching for her crayons to capture the scene on paper.

Jacob was tinkering with a remote-controlled car, his fingers skillfully adjusting a tiny wheel. "Could use a solar panel on top," he muttered, half to himself, already envisioning the upgrade.

The friends, each absorbed in their own play, shared a bond that was as strong as the sturdiest oak on Maple Street. They were more than just neighbors; they were a team.

Their play was interrupted by Mr. Benson, the kindly mailman, whose arrival always seemed to bring more than just letters and packages. "Big news today, kids!" he announced, unfolding a message from the town council.

"What's up, Mr. Benson?" asked Leo, who instinctively felt this was a moment to gather around.

"The mayor himself is coming to our festival," said Mr. Benson, his eyes twinkling. "He hears Maple Street knows how to throw a party and wants to see for himself!"

The kids gasped and buzzed with excitement. The Maple Street Festival was always a highlight, but this year would be truly special.

"We need to do something awesome!" Leo declared, his mind racing with possibilities.

"Yes! Let's hold a mini-election and choose a 'Mayor of Maple Street'!" suggested Mia, her voice alive with enthusiasm.

"Great idea! The mayor of Maple Street could speak to the real mayor about our ideas," Jacob chimed in, already thinking of improvements for the neighborhood.

The kids laughed and agreed. The excitement was palpable. And before anyone could say another word, it was clear who they wanted as their leader.

"Leo, you should be our mayor!" the children cheered, and although Leo felt a flutter of nerves, he knew he had to accept. He cared too much for Maple Street and the people within it to let this opportunity slip by.

As the impromptu ceremony came to a close and promises of grand plans filled the air, none of them could have predicted the adventures that lay ahead. This was the beginning of something wonderful; this was the start of Leo's journey as the Mayor of Maple Street.
With the unofficial title now bestowed upon him, Leo felt a surge of responsibility. "Alright, team," he started, "Let's meet tomorrow after school and brainstorm. We've got a festival to plan!"

And so, the very next day, under the watchful limbs of the old tree, the children of Maple Street gathered with eagerness in their eyes and ideas bubbling in their minds.

"I think we should make banners!" Mia proposed, her sketchpad filled with colorful designs. "We can hang them all along Maple Street. It will be like a rainbow exploded over us!"

"I like that!" Leo said, nodding enthusiastically. "And Jacob, do you think you could build something cool—something that shows what the future of Maple Street might look like?"

Jacob's eyes sparkled with excitement. "I could build a model of the street—add a mini park, and maybe even a place where animals could come to visit!"

The ideas came thick and fast, each child voicing their thoughts while Leo did his best to jot them down. They would plant flowers, set up game booths, and have a bake sale with treats no one could resist.

"So much to do," Leo mused, feeling the weight of leadership bearing down on his shoulders. He gazed at the list, which had grown long and unruly. "Okay, let's split up and get to work!"

As Mia and some of her artistic friends set up a crafting station for the banners, Leo worked with Jacob on logistics for the model town. But soon, Leo found himself darting from group to group, checking in, offering advice, and making decisions. He was everywhere all at once, and at first, it seemed to work.

Yet, as days passed, the initial excitement began to give way to fatigue. Leo was running out of breath, his presence at every project becoming less about fun and more about efficiency.

"We have to make sure everything's perfect," Leo insisted one afternoon as Mia frowned at her half-finished banner. "We can't let the mayor think we're just a bunch of kids playing around. This has to look professional."

Mia put down her paintbrush. "But Leo, it's not about being perfect. It's about having fun and showing how amazing Maple Street is."

Leo paused, considering her words, but there was no time. The festival was almost upon them, and there was still so much to do. "Don't worry, Mia. It'll be fun. Just trust me."

In his zest to be the best mayor Maple Street could have, Leo gradually stopped asking for input, making snap decisions that, while expeditious, weren't always in tune with what his friends wanted. The pressure was building, and shadows of doubt crept into the sunny days that led up to the mayor's arrival.

As the festival drew near, the streets lined with half-finished banners and a model town still under construction, tension among the children of Maple Street was at an all-time high. It all came to a head when Jacob's carefully built model town, a miniature version of their beloved neighborhood, collapsed in a heap of cardboard and glue.

"No!" Jacob exclaimed, staring at the ruins of what was once his contribution to the festival. "Who touched it? It was fine just a minute ago!"

"I just leaned against the table, that's all!" protested one of the younger kids, his voice quivering with worry.

"There's no time for this!" Leo's voice rose above the commotion. "We have to fix this, and fast. Jacob, start rebuilding. I'll get the glue."

"But Leo," Mia interjected, her own banner lying forgotten, "you're not even listening to him. We're all stressed, and it was just an accident."

Leo, his focus narrowed to tasks and to-do lists, barely glanced her way. "We don't have time for accidents or discussions. We need results!"

The group worked in silence, the joyous camaraderie from just days before replaced with a frantic urgency. Mia delicately dabbed at her streaky banners, struggling to match her earlier work's vibrancy. The swift brush strokes felt hollow, devoid of the shared laughter that usually accompanied their creation.

Jacob tried to piece together the remains of the model town, but his hands shook, and the glue wouldn't hold. Pieces that had fit so effortlessly before now seemed awkward and out of place. He couldn't help but notice Leo's sharp, cajoling tone in the background, pushing everyone beyond their limits.

Leo stood in the middle of the chaos he had unwittingly directed. He looked around and finally saw the upset faces of his friends. The vibrancy of Maple Street had dimmed, the excitement seemed drained. A hollow victory at the festival seemed inevitable. It was a stark contrast to the community spirit they all cherished.

That night, Leo lay in bed staring at the ceiling, the laughter and joy of Maple Street playing like a distant melody in his mind. He thought about Mia's forgotten passion, Jacob's shattered creation, and the unity that had been the street's beating heart.

What had he done? In his attempt to make the festival perfect, he'd forgotten the most important part – his friends. It wasn't just about winning or impressing the mayor. It was about their community, their shared experiences, and their friendship. A knot formed in Leo's throat.

"I've got to make this right," Leo whispered into the quiet room. As he finally drifted off to sleep, a plan began to take shape, one that he hoped would mend the fabric of their friendship and restore the heart of Maple Street.

The morning sun cascaded through the leaves of the old tree, casting dappled shadows across the faces of the children gathered below. They looked up as Leo approached, a determined yet humble look in his eyes.

"Friends," Leo began, his voice soft but clear, "I have something important to say. I've made a mistake. I got so caught up in making things perfect for the festival that I forgot what makes Maple Street really special – it's us, working together, enjoying each other's company. I'm sorry."

The children exchanged glances, the previous day's tensions lingering like morning dew. Mia set aside her paintbrush, her gaze meeting Leo's. "We all wanted the festival to be great, Leo. But you're right, it's not just about the decorations or impressing the mayor. We forgot to have fun."

Jacob stepped forward, a supportive smile breaking through. "Yeah, and the best part of Maple Street is how we all help each other. Let's rebuild the model town together – as a team."

And that's exactly what they did. With Leo's encouragement, everyone pitched in, bringing their own ideas and flair to the project. The model town came back to life, this time not as a showpiece for one person's skill, but as a patchwork of imagination from all the kids on Maple Street.

The banners, too, were transformed. Now each one bore the strokes, doodles, and handprints of a dozen children, each telling a story of joy and collective effort. The street was alive with the sound of laughter and collaboration.

When the mayor arrived, he was greeted not by a street striving for perfection, but one bursting with life and color. The children, all smiles and welcome, shared stories of their work and the fun they had putting everything together.

"This is truly impressive," the mayor remarked, his eyes twinkling with delight. "I can see that the spirit of Maple Street isn't just in the decorations, it's in its people – especially its youngest members."

The festival was a hit, not because it was flawless, but because it was a true reflection of the community and the hearts of those who lived there.

As the children basked in the glow of a job well done, Leo knew that he had learned a valuable lesson. It wasn't about being in charge or making everything just so; it was about listening, really listening, to what those around him had to say. Leadership was about bringing out the best in everyone and making sure that, above all, they were together in their efforts.

So as the sun set and the stars began to peek through the evening sky, Leo, the Mayor of Maple Street, and all his friends knew that they had crafted more than just a successful festival – they had woven a memory of friendship and unity that would long outlast any decoration or model town.

In the heart of the Silent Forest, where whispers of magic danced with the wind, Jake and his cousin Emma embarked on an adventure they would never forget. The forest was a tapestry of vibrant greens and soft, dappled sunlight that played hide and seek among the leaves.

"Look at this place, Emma! It's like something out of a fairy tale," exclaimed Jake, his eyes sparkling with excitement as he gazed at the towering trees and the colorful birds flitting between the branches.

Emma, with a curious glint in her eyes, nodded in agreement. "It's beautiful, Jake. But remember, we're here for more than just sightseeing. There's a secret hidden in this forest, and I bet we're the ones who'll find it."

As they ventured deeper, the forest seemed to welcome them with open arms, its air filled with the sweet scent of wildflowers and the soft rustling of leaves. They came across an old, wise-looking man with a gentle smile, sitting on a fallen log.

"Ah, young explorers," he greeted them, his voice as calm as the forest itself. "What brings you to the Silent Forest?"

"We've heard about a secret hidden here," Jake replied eagerly. "And we're going to find it!"

The old man chuckled softly. "The forest holds many secrets, some as old as time itself. But remember, the forest only reveals its secrets to those who are worthy."

"What do you mean, 'worthy'?" Emma asked, her curiosity piqued.

"A true seeker of the forest's secrets must show bravery, wisdom, and a respectful heart. Only then will the forest unveil its mysteries," the old man answered, his eyes twinkling mysteriously.

Jake and Emma exchanged excited glances. "We accept the challenge!" Jake declared.

The old man smiled and handed them a small, intricately carved wooden box. "This box holds the first clue to your adventure. Solve its riddle, and you shall be one step closer to uncovering the forest's secret."

Taking the box, Jake and Emma noticed it had symbols and letters etched into its surface. They knew this was the beginning of something extraordinary.

As the old man vanished into the shadows of the trees, the cousins sat down on the soft forest floor, surrounded by the gentle sounds of nature. They examined the box closely, their minds racing with possibilities.

"Do you think we can really find the secret, Jake?" Emma asked, her voice filled with a mix of excitement and uncertainty.

Jake looked at her with determined eyes. "We can and we will. This is our adventure, Emma. Let's solve this mystery together!"

With the spirit of adventure in their hearts and the mystery of the Silent Forest calling to them, Jake and Emma began their quest, unaware of the incredible journey that lay ahead.
Jake and Emma studied the wooden box, their fingers tracing the intricate carvings. The symbols seemed to form a pattern, a puzzle waiting to be solved.

"Look, these symbols, they're not just random. They form a path!" Emma pointed out excitedly.

"You're right! It's like a map," Jake agreed, his eyes lighting up. "I think it's showing us a way deeper into the forest."

With renewed determination, they followed the clues from the box, each symbol guiding them further into the heart of the Silent Forest. The deeper they went, the more enchanting the forest became. Vines hung like curtains from the trees, and flowers with luminous petals lined their path.

As they journeyed, they encountered a series of challenges. First, a river with waters as clear as crystal blocked their path. The only way across was a series of stepping stones that appeared and disappeared, as if playing a game with the travelers.

"Watch the pattern, Emma!" Jake called out as he carefully stepped onto a stone, only to have it vanish beneath him, causing him to leap to the next one.

Emma followed, her nimble feet barely touching the stones as they made their way across. "This forest is full of surprises," she laughed, her voice echoing through the trees.

Their next challenge was a great wall of thorns, stretching high and wide with no apparent way through. But upon closer inspection, Jake noticed that the thorns moved ever so slightly, creating a narrow path.

"It's like a maze," he said, leading the way. "We need to be careful and think about each step."

They weaved through the thorny maze, ducking and dodging the sharp branches. It was a test of their agility and patience, but together, they emerged on the other side, unscathed.

"That was intense," Emma gasped, brushing a leaf from her hair. "What's next?"

As if in answer to her question, they stumbled upon a clearing where a majestic owl perched on a tree stump. Its eyes seemed to pierce right through them.

"The forest guardian," Jake whispered in awe.

The owl spoke in a voice that was both eerie and wise. "To reach the heart of the forest, one must answer my riddle. Fail, and you shall go no further."

Jake and Emma listened intently as the owl presented its riddle. It was a puzzle that twisted and turned, a play on words and nature's lore. They huddled together, whispering and debating, their minds racing through the possibilities.

Finally, Emma's face lit up. "I've got it, Jake! The answer is…"

As she spoke the answer, the owl nodded, its eyes softening. "Wise and brave, you have proven yourselves. The path to the forest's heart is now open."

A path lit up, glowing softly, leading them deeper into the Silent Forest. Jake and Emma, filled with excitement and a sense of achievement, continued their journey, unaware that the biggest challenge still awaited them. The forest whispered secrets around them, its magic growing stronger with every step they took towards the unknown.

The glowing path led Jake and Emma to a clearing where the air thrummed with a strange, ancient energy. In the center stood an old tree, its bark inscribed with symbols that shimmered under the moonlight. At its base lay a stone pedestal with a hollowed-out top, as if waiting for something to be placed within it.

"This must be it, the heart of the forest!" Emma whispered, her eyes wide with awe.

Jake approached the tree cautiously. "There's one last puzzle to solve, I think. Look at these symbols. They're similar to the ones on the box."

The cousins circled the tree, studying the symbols. Each symbol seemed to represent an element of the forest - a leaf, a drop of water, a flame, and a gust of wind.

"We need to find these elements and bring them here," Jake concluded.

Splitting up, they ventured back into the forest. Emma found a leaf from the rarest tree, glowing with a soft, green light. Jake captured a droplet of dew from the most elusive flower, shimmering like a diamond. Together, they found a flame from a firefly and a gust of wind trapped inside a bubble.

They returned to the tree, placing each element into the hollow of the pedestal. As they did, the symbols on the tree glowed brighter, and the ground beneath their feet began to tremble.

Suddenly, a deep voice echoed through the forest. It was the Mysterious Old Man, now standing before them. "You have done well to reach this far. But the final test is the most crucial. You must prove that your hearts are pure and that you can bear the secret of the Silent Forest."

The tree's roots began to rise, forming an archway. Beyond it, a brilliant light shone, beckoning them forward.

"This is it, Emma. We're so close," Jake said, taking a deep breath.

Hand in hand, they stepped through the archway. The light enveloped them, and for a moment, everything was calm and bright. Then, images flashed before their eyes - the history of the forest, its joys, and sorrows, its birth, and growth. They saw the forest in all its glory and understood its true significance.

As the light faded, they found themselves back in the clearing. The Old Man smiled. "You have seen the heart of the forest and understood its essence. The secret is safe with you."

Jake and Emma, overwhelmed by the experience, nodded solemnly. They realized the forest was more than just trees and wildlife; it was a living, breathing entity that needed to be respected and protected.

"You are now the guardians of the Silent Forest," the Old Man declared. "Remember, with great knowledge comes great responsibility."

As the first rays of dawn broke through the trees, the cousins knew their adventure was over, but their journey as guardians had just begun. They stepped out of the forest, forever changed, carrying with them the secret of the Silent Forest.

As Jake and Emma emerged from the Silent Forest, the world outside seemed brighter, filled with new colors and sounds. They walked in silence, each lost in thought about the incredible journey they had just completed.

"It feels like we've been in a whole different world," Emma finally said, looking back at the forest. "Do you think anyone will believe our story?"

Jake smiled. "It doesn't matter if they do or not. We know what happened, and we have a responsibility now."

As they walked, they talked about the lessons they had learned. They realized that leadership wasn't just about seeking adventures and solving mysteries. It was about understanding the importance of what you find and protecting it.

"When we first entered the forest, all I could think about was finding the secret," Jake confessed. "But now, I realize it's not just about finding something. It's about what you do with what you find."

Emma nodded. "And respecting what we don't understand. The forest has its secrets for a reason. We were lucky to see them, but we need to keep them safe."

Their conversation was interrupted by the Mysterious Old Man, who appeared one last time on their path. "You have both grown in more ways than you know," he said, his voice filled with pride. "The forest has chosen wisely in its guardians."

He handed them each a small pendant, shaped like a leaf. "These will remind you of your journey and your promise. Remember, the forest is always a part of you, and you are a part of it."

Jake and Emma thanked the Old Man, and with a final nod, he disappeared, leaving them alone on the path.

As they neared home, they looked at each other, a sense of understanding passing between them. They had started this adventure as cousins, but now they were partners, guardians of a magical secret.

Back home, their families were surprised at how mature and thoughtful they had become. Jake and Emma shared stories of their adventure, leaving out the magical parts, of course. But whenever they touched their pendants, they remembered the Silent Forest and the lessons it taught them.

The story of Jake and Emma's adventure in the Silent Forest became a favorite tale in their family. It was a story of bravery, intelligence, and respect for nature. But most importantly, it was a story about how true leadership involves uncovering truths, solving mysteries, and above all, protecting those secrets for the greater good.

As Jake and Emma grew older, they often returned to the edge of the Silent Forest, remembering their adventure and the promise they made. They knew that the forest would always be there, silent and wise, holding its secrets close, just as they held theirs.

The school corridors buzzed with excitement, bursting with colorful posters and catchy slogans that decorated every wall. In the midst of this vibrant scene was Alex, his eyes shining with a mix of nervousness and excitement. He clutched a stack of handmade posters, each one carefully crafted with bright colors and bold words: "Vote for Alex - Let's Make a Difference!"

"Hey Alex, those posters look awesome!" exclaimed Mia, one of his classmates, as she passed by.

"Thanks, Mia! I worked on them all weekend," Alex replied, a proud smile spreading across his face.

In the classroom, Mrs. Lee, the teacher overseeing the elections, was discussing the importance of student council. "It's not just about planning fun events," she said, "It's about leadership, responsibility, and giving everyone a voice."

Alex listened intently, his mind racing with ideas. He had always wanted to make a difference in his school, and this was his chance.

After class, Alex approached Mrs. Lee. "I've decided to run for student council," he said, his voice a mix of determination and hesitation.

"That's wonderful, Alex!" Mrs. Lee responded warmly. "Remember, it's about honesty and your vision for our school."

Outside, Alex began hanging his posters, carefully placing them next to the flashy ones of his competitors, Sophia and Dylan. Sophia, known for her clever ideas, had digital posters that changed colors. Dylan, popular and charismatic, had posters with his picture and a catchy slogan: "Dylan for Action!"

As Alex was taping up his last poster, Dylan walked over with a smirk. "Nice posters, Alex. But it takes more than that to win an election," he said, oozing confidence.

Alex felt a twinge of doubt but quickly brushed it off. "It's not just about winning, Dylan. It's about making our school better," he replied firmly.

Sophia joined them, eyeing the posters. "May the best campaign win," she said with a sly smile, before heading off.

The next day, the school was abuzz with election talk. In the playground, groups of students discussed who they would vote for. Alex joined a group of his friends, who were eager to hear his ideas.

"I want to create a recycling program and organize more outdoor activities," Alex shared enthusiastically.

"That sounds cool!" said one of his friends, "I'm tired of the same old stuff."

Alex's heart swelled with hope. This was more than just an election; it was a chance to bring positive change to his school. With each passing day, his excitement grew, but so did the challenges. He knew this journey wouldn't be easy, but he was ready to give it his all, with fairness and integrity at the heart of his campaign.

The campaign was in full swing, and every corner of the school seemed to echo with election fever. Alex spent every spare moment he had talking to classmates, explaining his ideas, and answering questions. He felt a thrill every time someone said they'd consider voting for him.

In the lunchroom, Alex overheard Sophia discussing her latest campaign idea. "I'm planning a 'Sophia's Science Fun Day'. It'll show everyone how fun learning can be!" she said to a group of wide-eyed students.

Alex admired Sophia's creativity but worried that his own ideas might seem less exciting in comparison.

Later, in the playground, Alex watched Dylan charm a group of students with his charisma. "Vote for me, and I promise the coolest school year ever!" Dylan boasted, high-fiving his supporters.

Feeling a bit discouraged, Alex returned to his classroom. Mrs. Lee noticed his gloomy expression and asked, "Is everything okay, Alex?"

Alex nodded, trying to stay positive. "It's just that Sophia and Dylan have such great campaigns. I'm not sure if my ideas are enough."

Mrs. Lee smiled kindly. "Alex, it's not about flashy ideas. It's about what you believe in and the difference you can make. Stay true to yourself."

Buoyed by Mrs. Lee's words, Alex decided to organize a small event to showcase his ideas. He arranged a meeting in the school library and invited his classmates to discuss his recycling initiative and outdoor activity plans.

To his delight, the meeting was a success. Many students were excited about his ideas, especially the recycling program. "We could even have a competition to see which class recycles the most each month!" suggested one student.

Alex's spirits lifted as he realized his ideas resonated with his classmates. But the campaign trail wasn't without its challenges.

One afternoon, while Alex was putting up some new posters, he overheard a conversation that stopped him in his tracks. A group of students were discussing a rumor that Alex was planning to cancel some beloved school events if he won.

Confused and hurt, Alex approached the group. "That's not true at all. I don't know where that rumor came from, but it's completely false," he explained earnestly.

The students seemed relieved but Alex was shaken. He had a strong suspicion that Dylan was behind the rumors, but he had no proof.

Determined not to let this setback defeat him, Alex focused even more on his campaign, speaking passionately about his vision for the school and addressing any rumors head-on with honesty and clarity.

As the election day drew nearer, the tension was palpable. Alex felt a mix of excitement and nerves. He knew the outcome was uncertain, but he was proud of the campaign he had run. He had stayed true to himself and his values, no matter what challenges came his way.

As election day loomed, the rumors and tension reached a peak. Alex, feeling the strain, decided it was time to address the situation head-on. He requested to speak at the school assembly, a platform where he could reach all his classmates at once. Mrs. Lee, sensing the importance of the moment, agreed.

The auditorium buzzed with whispers as Alex stepped onto the stage. His heart pounded, but his voice was steady. "I know there have been rumors about me wanting to cancel some of our favorite school events," he began. "I want everyone to know that these rumors are completely false. My goal is to add more activities, not take them away."

The audience listened intently. Alex's sincerity was evident. "This election should be about ideas and making our school better, not about spreading false rumors," he continued. "I believe in honesty and fair play, and I hope whoever wins will hold those values too."

As Alex concluded, the auditorium erupted in applause. Students who had been swayed by the rumors now looked at him with newfound respect.

Later that day, Dylan approached Alex in the hallway. "I heard your speech," Dylan said, avoiding eye contact. "Look, I... I may have let things get too competitive."

Alex was surprised but appreciative of Dylan's admission. "Thanks for saying that, Dylan. Let's both try to make this a fair election, no matter what."

Election day arrived, and the school was abuzz with anticipation. Alex felt a mix of nervousness and pride. He had run a campaign he believed in, staying true to his principles. Whether he won or lost, he knew he had made a positive impact.

In the auditorium, Mrs. Lee stood on stage with an envelope in her hand. "I'm proud of all our candidates," she announced. "You've shown creativity, passion, and resilience. Now, let's see who our new student council members are."

The room fell silent as Mrs. Lee read the names. Alex held his breath, waiting. Then, his name was called. He had won a seat on the student council.

The crowd cheered, and Alex's friends rushed to congratulate him. He looked over and saw Dylan clapping, a genuine smile on his face. Sophia came over, too, offering her congratulations.

"Great job, Alex. You're going to be an awesome council member," she said warmly.

As the assembly ended, Alex felt a wave of relief and excitement. He had overcome the challenges and emerged stronger. He realized that the true victory wasn't just winning the election; it was staying true to himself and his values, proving that integrity and fairness really do matter.

The school halls were filled with a new kind of energy following the elections. Alex, now a member of the student council, was busy planning his first initiative. He was determined to make his term meaningful and impactful.

One afternoon, while Alex was discussing his recycling program plans with some classmates, Mrs. Lee approached him. "Alex, can I have a word with you?" she asked with a smile.

"Of course, Mrs. Lee," Alex replied, curious.

"I just wanted to say how proud I am of you," she began. "You faced challenges in this election, but you handled them with integrity and grace. You're a true leader."

Alex beamed, feeling a sense of accomplishment. "Thank you, Mrs. Lee. I learned that it's not just about winning; it's about how you play the game."

"Exactly," Mrs. Lee agreed. "And you played it well."

In the following weeks, Alex worked hard on the council. He helped implement the recycling program, which was a big hit with students and teachers alike. He also organized a series of outdoor educational activities, which brought a fresh burst of excitement to the school.

One day, while overseeing a recycling competition, Alex was joined by Dylan. "Hey, Alex. The recycling program's really taking off, huh?" Dylan said, looking around at the busy students.

"Yeah, it's going better than I hoped," Alex replied, happy to see Dylan taking an interest.

"I wanted to apologize again for the rumors during the election," Dylan said sincerely. "I learned a lot from you about playing fair. I'm thinking of helping out with the school's sports events to make sure they're fun and fair for everyone."

"That's a great idea, Dylan," Alex responded, genuinely impressed.

Sophia joined them, her eyes bright with enthusiasm. "I'm planning a new science club. I was wondering if you'd like to collaborate? Your outdoor activities would be a perfect fit," she proposed.

"I'd love to," Alex said, excited by the prospect of working together.

As the school year progressed, Alex realized that the true victory wasn't just about holding a position on the student council. It was about the lessons learned and the friendships formed. He had shown his school the importance of integrity, honesty, and fair play. These values had not only guided him through the election but had also earned him the respect and trust of his peers.

Sitting in the school garden one sunny afternoon, Alex reflected on his journey. He had faced challenges but had stayed true to his values. He had learned that winning is important, but how you win is what truly defines you. With this realization, Alex knew that no matter what the future held, he was ready to face it with the same fairness and integrity that had guided him through the great school election.

Beyond the blue skies of Earth, amidst the vast expanse of space, a sleek spaceship glided towards its destination: Mars. Inside the spacecraft, Ethan, a boy with eyes full of dreams and a heart brimming with courage, gazed out at the stars. He was not alone on this grand adventure; his fellow astronauts, Ava and Raj, were with him, each equally thrilled and anxious about their mission.

"Can you believe it? We're actually going to land on Mars!" Ethan exclaimed, his voice echoing in the compact cabin.

Ava, with her sharp, observant eyes, nodded in agreement. "It's like something out of a sci-fi movie, but it's real! I can't wait to conduct experiments on the Martian soil."

Raj, always the joker, grinned and added, "And here I am, just excited about zero-gravity snacks. But seriously, it's going to be an epic journey."

Their spacecraft was a marvel of technology, equipped with everything they needed for their mission. The interior was a labyrinth of computers, buttons, and screens, all blinking and whirring in harmony.

As they neared Mars, the red planet loomed large and mysterious before them. Its surface, a tapestry of crimson and rust, was mesmerizing. The excitement in the cabin was palpable as they prepared for landing.

Suddenly, a warning light flashed on the dashboard. Ethan's heart skipped a beat. "What's happening?" he asked, trying to keep his voice steady.

Ava, who was monitoring the control panel, replied, "It looks like a meteor shower. It's small but heading our way fast!"

Raj quickly joined Ava at the controls. "We need to adjust our course," he said urgently.

Working together, they maneuvered the spaceship, dodging the streaks of light that were the meteors blazing past them. Ethan watched, his hands clenched, as Ava and Raj skillfully navigated through the cosmic storm.

"That was too close," Ethan breathed out as the last of the meteors passed by.

Ava checked the instruments. "We've got some minor damage to the hull, but we should still be able to land."

Raj let out a long whistle. "Talk about an exciting start to our mission, huh?"

Ethan smiled, his confidence returning. "We made it through, thanks to you two. Mars, here we come!"

As the spaceship descended towards the Martian surface, the three astronauts braced themselves. They were about to step into the unknown, ready to face whatever challenges lay ahead, together. The adventure of a lifetime was just beginning.

The spaceship gently touched down on the Martian surface, kicking up clouds of red dust. The trio exchanged excited glances as they prepared to step out into this new world. Ethan was the first to emerge, his boots making contact with the alien soil. "We're actually walking on Mars!" he exclaimed in awe.

Ava followed, her eyes wide with wonder. "It's so... different. Look at the sky, it's not blue like Earth's!"

"And much quieter too," Raj observed, joining them outside. "Okay, team, let's start our exploration. Remember, safety first."

They ventured forth, their suits protecting them from the harsh Martian environment. Their mission was to collect soil samples and search for signs of past water. As they worked, they chatted about everything they saw, their voices crackling over the radio.

"Hey, look at this rock formation!" Ethan pointed to a cluster of jagged rocks. "It looks like it's been shaped by water."

Ava knelt down beside him, examining the rocks. "You might be right, Ethan. This could be a major discovery!"

Their exploration took them farther from the spaceship, into a landscape filled with towering canyons and vast plains. The Martian surface was a mystery waiting to be unraveled, and they were the ones to do it.

As the day progressed, Raj noticed something unusual on his scanner. "Guys, check this out. I'm getting some weird readings from that direction." He pointed towards a distant mountain.

"What kind of readings?" Ava asked, intrigued.

"It's hard to tell, but it's definitely not natural. It's like a pulsating energy signal," Raj explained.

Ethan's curiosity was piqued. "Let's go check it out. It could be something important."

They changed course, heading towards the source of the signal. The terrain grew more challenging, with steep slopes and loose rocks. Despite the obstacles, they pressed on, driven by the mystery ahead.

As they neared the mountain, they noticed a faint, pulsating light emanating from a cave entrance. It was unlike anything they had seen before.

"Wow, what is that?" Ethan whispered, his eyes fixed on the glowing entrance.

Ava adjusted her equipment. "I don't know, but we should be careful. We don't know what's inside."

Raj nodded in agreement. "Let's approach slowly. Keep your communicators on, and if anything happens, we head back to the ship immediately."

They crept towards the cave, their hearts racing with anticipation and a hint of fear. The light grew brighter as they approached, casting eerie shadows on the cave walls. Inside, the light pulsed rhythmically, beckoning them further.

Little did they know, their biggest challenge was just around the corner, a challenge that would test their bravery and teamwork to the fullest.
As they ventured deeper into the cave, the pulsating light grew more intense, its rhythm almost hypnotic. The walls of the cave were lined with crystals that glowed softly, adding to the surreal atmosphere.

"This is incredible," Ava breathed, her voice filled with wonder. "These crystals might be the source of the energy signal."

Ethan was about to respond when suddenly, a loud rumbling echoed through the cave. Startled, they turned to see a cloud of red dust billowing towards them from the entrance.

"A sandstorm!" Raj shouted. "We need to get out of here, now!"

They hurried back towards the entrance, but the storm was upon them faster than they anticipated. In the chaos, Ethan tripped over a rock and fell behind. "Go on without me! I'll catch up!" he yelled over the howling wind.

Ava and Raj hesitated, but the storm was too fierce. Trusting Ethan's word, they made their way out of the cave, struggling against the relentless Martian wind.

Outside, the storm raged, reducing visibility to almost zero. Ava and Raj managed to find shelter behind a large boulder, catching their breath.

"We have to go back for Ethan," Ava said, determination in her eyes.

Raj nodded. "As soon as the storm lets up, we'll go find him."

Meanwhile, Ethan, still inside the cave, fought to stand up. His leg hurt, but he knew he couldn't stay there. Using the cave wall for support, he started to make his way out, calling for his friends.

"Ava! Raj!" His voice was lost in the roar of the storm.

Outside, the storm finally began to subside, revealing a Martian landscape blanketed in red dust. Ava and Raj, worried and anxious, ventured back towards the cave.

"Ethan!" they called, their voices echoing in the emptiness.

Back in the cave, Ethan heard his name and quickened his pace, despite the pain. As he neared the entrance, he saw the silhouettes of Ava and Raj against the bright Martian sky.

"There he is!" Raj exclaimed, relief flooding his voice.

Ava rushed to Ethan's side, helping him out of the cave. "Are you okay?"

"I twisted my ankle, but I'll manage," Ethan replied, trying to mask his discomfort.

Together, they made their way back to their spaceship, leaning on each other for support. The sun was setting on Mars, casting a golden glow over the landscape. Despite the challenges they faced, they felt a deep sense of accomplishment and camaraderie.

As they reached their spaceship, Ethan looked back at the mountain and the cave. They had faced the unknown and emerged stronger. He knew this was an experience they would never forget, a testament to their bravery and unbreakable bond.

Back in the safety of their spaceship, Ethan, Ava, and Raj tended to Ethan's injury. As they sat together, the spaceship began its journey back to Earth, leaving Mars behind.

"We did it, team," Ethan said with a smile, his ankle bandaged. "We explored Mars and found something incredible."

Ava nodded, her eyes shining with pride. "And we faced challenges we never expected. I'm glad we had each other."

Raj, who was checking the data they had collected, added, "This mission was more than just exploring Mars. We learned how important it is to trust and support each other."

As the spaceship cruised through space, the trio spent their time reviewing their findings and sharing stories of their adventure. The pulsating light in the cave remained a mystery, but they had gathered enough data for scientists back on Earth to study.

Ethan gazed out the window at the stars, deep in thought. "You know, when that sandstorm hit, and I was alone in the cave, I was really scared. But knowing you both were out there, waiting for me, gave me the strength to keep going."

Ava put a hand on his shoulder. "That's what friends do, Ethan. We stick together, no matter what."

Raj chimed in, "Exactly! And think about the story we'll have to tell. We're probably the first kids to get caught in a Martian sandstorm!"

They all laughed, the sound echoing warmly in the cabin.

As Earth came into view, a beautiful blue orb against the blackness of space, the magnitude of their journey struck them. They had traveled to another planet, faced unforeseen dangers, and returned safely, all because they worked together as a team.

The spaceship touched down on Earth, welcomed by cheers and applause. Their families and friends were there to greet them, along with a crowd of people eager to hear about their adventure.

As they stepped out of the spaceship, Ethan, Ava, and Raj were hailed as heroes. But for them, the greatest achievement was not the fame or the successful mission; it was the unbreakable bond they had formed and the lessons they had learned.

Ethan, Ava, and Raj stood together, facing the crowd. Ethan spoke up, "We went to Mars as a team, and we returned as a team. We learned that bravery isn't just about facing dangers, but also about trusting and helping each other. Our expedition to Mars taught us the true power of friendship and teamwork."

Their story of courage, friendship, and teamwork became an inspiration to children all over the world. And as for Ethan, Ava, and Raj, they knew this was just the beginning of many more adventures to come.

In a little town where the extraordinary often happened, Ryan and his sister Lily lived a life filled with wonder and curiosity. Their backyard was their sanctuary, a place where imaginations ran as wild as the wind.

One sunny afternoon, while playing hide and seek, Ryan stumbled upon a hidden pathway, cloaked in ivy and mystery. "Lily, come quickly!" he shouted, excitement ringing in his voice.

Lily, with her sharp, inquisitive eyes, dashed over. "What is it, Ryan?"

"I've found something amazing!" Ryan's eyes sparkled with the thrill of discovery. Together, they pushed through the overgrown foliage, and to their astonishment, found themselves standing at the threshold of a world unlike any other. It was a land where the trees soared into the clouds and the flowers were as big as umbrellas.

"This place is incredible!" gasped Lily, her voice a mix of awe and disbelief.

"It's like a giant's world," Ryan whispered, his gaze wandering over the colossal landscape.

No sooner had the words left his mouth, than a shadow loomed over them. Heartbeats racing, they slowly turned to see a giant standing tall and proud. He was as large as a house, with eyes as gentle as the morning sky.

"Don't be afraid," the giant said in a voice that rumbled like distant thunder. "I am Gulliver, guardian of this land."

Ryan, though initially frightened, found courage. "We mean no harm, Gulliver. I'm Ryan and this is my sister, Lily. We found this place by accident."

Gulliver smiled, a warm, inviting smile. "Accidents often lead to the greatest adventures. You have entered the land of giants, a place of magic and untold mysteries."

Lily, overcoming her initial shock, stepped forward. "What kind of mysteries?"

Gulliver's eyes twinkled. "There is a challenge, one that has remained unsolved for ages. A rare crystal, hidden deep within the enchanted forest. It holds the power to enlighten one with the true essence of leadership and bravery."

Ryan's heart leaped. An adventure, a real one, was unfolding before him. "Can we help? Can we find this crystal?"

Gulliver nodded. "Yes, but it won't be easy. The path is filled with puzzles and perils. It requires courage, wit, and a strong heart."

"We'll do it!" Ryan declared, his voice ringing with determination. Lily nodded in agreement, her eyes alight with the thrill of the challenge.

"Very well," Gulliver said. "Follow the trail of silver leaves, and it will lead you to the edge of the enchanted forest. That is where your quest will begin."

With hearts full of excitement and minds racing with possibilities, Ryan and Lily embarked on their journey, stepping into a world of giants, and towards an adventure that would test their courage like never before.

As Ryan and Lily ventured deeper into the land of giants, they found themselves on a path lined with shimmering silver leaves, each leaf larger than a dinner plate. The forest around them was alive with sounds of mysterious creatures and rustling trees.

"Look at these footprints!" Lily pointed to a set of enormous indents in the earth. "They're huge!"

"They must be from one of the giants," Ryan said, his eyes wide with wonder.

Their path led them to a clearing where a giant root maze stretched out before them. The roots twisted and turned, creating a labyrinth that seemed impossible to navigate.

"We'll need to work together to get through this," Ryan said, examining the maze.

Lily nodded, her mind already racing with ideas. "Let's use sticks to mark where we've been so we don't go in circles."

The siblings started the maze, turning left and right, marking their path. They encountered dead ends and had to retrace their steps, but slowly, they made progress. The maze tested their patience and teamwork, but together, they found their way to the other side.

Emerging from the maze, they were greeted by a group of mystical creatures, resembling small dragons with feathers instead of scales. The creatures fluttered around them, chirping in a language the children didn't understand.

"Are they trying to tell us something?" Lily wondered aloud.

Ryan watched the creatures closely. "I think they want us to follow them."

They followed the creatures to a river, where the water flowed in reverse, defying gravity. Across the river was their next path, but there was no bridge in sight.

"How do we cross this?" Lily asked, puzzled.

One of the feathered creatures flew over the river, dropping a pebble into the water. Where the pebble hit, a stepping stone appeared.

"It's a puzzle," Ryan realized. "We need to throw pebbles in the right order to create a path."

Taking turns, they tossed pebbles into the river, watching as stepping stones emerged from the water. It took several tries, and a few stones vanished when they guessed wrong, but eventually, a path of stones formed, allowing them to cross the river.

On the other side, they found themselves at the edge of the enchanted forest. The trees were so tall they seemed to touch the sky, and the air was filled with a soft, magical glow.

"The crystal must be somewhere in there," Ryan said, gazing into the forest.

Lily nodded, determination set in her features. "Let's go find it."

As they stepped into the enchanted forest, the atmosphere changed. The air became thicker, and the path ahead was shrouded in a misty veil. Strange eyes peeked from behind the trees, and eerie sounds echoed around them.

Despite the eerie surroundings, Ryan and Lily pressed on, knowing that the heart of their adventure, and their greatest challenge, lay somewhere ahead in the mystical depths of the enchanted forest.

Deep within the enchanted forest, the trees grew so close together that their branches wove a dark canopy overhead. Ryan and Lily found themselves in front of an ancient, moss-covered labyrinth. Its walls towered over them, and an unsettling silence hung in the air.

"This must be it," Ryan whispered, staring at the labyrinth's entrance. "The final challenge."

Lily nodded, gripping her brother's hand. "We can do this. Together."

As they stepped into the labyrinth, they heard a deep, resonant voice echo around them. "To find the crystal, you must first find yourselves. Three tasks you shall face, and only with wisdom, bravery, and unity shall you succeed."

The first task appeared before them as a riddle, etched into a stone tablet. Ryan read it aloud, "I speak without a mouth and hear without ears. I have no body, but I come alive with wind. What am I?"

Lily pondered for a moment. "It's an echo!"

They shouted together, and their voices echoed back, causing a section of the labyrinth wall to slide open, revealing the next path.

The second task was a room with two doors, each guarded by a stone statue. The voice boomed again, "One door leads forward, the other leads back. One guardian always lies, the other always speaks the truth."

Ryan approached the first statue. "If I asked the other guardian which door leads forward, what would they say?"

The statue replied, pointing to the left door. Ryan thought hard. "It's the right door. If he's lying, the truth is the other door. If he's telling the truth, the liar would point to the wrong door."

They opened the right door, and it led them deeper into the labyrinth.

The final task was the most daunting. They entered a large chamber where the crystal hovered in the air, surrounded by a swirling vortex of wind and light.

"The final test," the voice said. "Only a true leader, brave and wise, can tame the storm and claim the crystal."

Ryan stepped forward, feeling a surge of fear and excitement. "I think it's about facing our fears, not fighting them."

He closed his eyes, taking a deep breath, and reached out his hand towards the vortex. Instead of trying to fight the swirling winds, he let his calmness and confidence flow into his touch.

The vortex responded, its wild motion gradually calming until it was a gentle breeze, swirling around Ryan's hand. He grasped the crystal, and it glowed brightly, its light filling the chamber.

"We did it, Lily! We did it together!" Ryan exclaimed, the crystal secure in his hand.

Lily hugged her brother tightly. "You were amazing, Ryan."

As the chamber lit up with the crystal's light, the walls of the labyrinth began to dissolve around them, revealing a clear path back to the forest's edge. They had faced the challenges with courage and wisdom, and together, they had triumphed.

With the crystal in hand, Ryan and Lily emerged from the enchanted forest, the trees seeming to bow in reverence to their courage and wisdom. The land of giants, once shrouded in mystery, now felt like a familiar friend.

As they made their way back to Gulliver, the giant greeted them with a beaming smile. "You have succeeded where many have faltered. You have the crystal!"

Ryan held up the glowing crystal. "We faced the challenges together, and learned so much."

Gulliver knelt down, his eyes reflecting pride. "You have discovered the true essence of leadership and bravery. It's not about facing challenges alone, but about facing them with wisdom, unity, and a brave heart."

Lily, her eyes shining with the day's adventures, added, "And understanding that sometimes, the biggest challenges are the ones we create in our minds."

Gulliver handed them a small pouch. "As a token of our gratitude, take these seeds from our land. Plant them in your world, and let the magic of this place grow with you."

Ryan and Lily thanked Gulliver and promised to return someday. As they walked back to the hidden pathway, the silver leaves rustled in the wind, as if waving goodbye.

Back in their backyard, they planted the seeds, covering them with the gentle care of newfound wisdom. The seeds took root, and small shoots sprang up, a reminder of their incredible journey.

That night, as they lay in bed, Ryan turned to his sister. "You know, Lily, I learned something important today. Being brave doesn't mean you're not afraid. It means you overcome your fear to do what's right."

Lily smiled, her eyes closing sleepily. "And being a leader isn't about being in charge. It's about taking care of those around you and facing challenges together."

As they drifted off to sleep, their dreams were filled with giants and enchanted forests, echoing with the laughter and lessons of their adventure.

In the days that followed, the plants from the giant's land grew, intertwining with the trees in their backyard, a living tapestry of their journey. Ryan and Lily often sat near them, reminded of the land of giants, where they learned the true meaning of bravery and leadership.

Their adventure in the land of giants became a cherished memory, a story they would tell for years to come. It was a journey that had not only changed the landscape of their backyard but had also changed them, teaching them that together, with courage and wisdom, they could face any challenge that came their way.

CONCLUSION

As the final page of "Courageous Stories - Shaping Boys into Leaders" come to a close, we hope these tales have ignited a spark of bravery, wisdom, and leadership in your hearts.

Remember, every great leader started as a learner, just like you, full of dreams and potential.

Carry these stories with you as you embark on your own adventures, and may your journey be as courageous and inspiring as those of the heroes you've just met.